BE

BE

PATRIA RIVERA

Carolyn Marie Souaid, Editor

Signature
EDITIONS

Cover design by Doowah Design.
Photo of Patria Rivera by Mónica Millán.

This book was printed on Ancient Forest Friendly paper.
Printed and bound in Canada by Marquis Book Printing Inc.

We acknowledge the support of The Canada Council for the Arts and the Manitoba Arts Council for our publishing program.

Library and Archives Canada Cataloguing in Publication

Rivera, Patria
        Be / Patria Rivera.

Poems.
ISBN 978-1-897109-52-6

        I. Title.

PS8635.I843B4 2011   C811'.6   C2011-902255-9

Signature Editions
P.O. Box 206, RPO Corydon, Winnipeg, Manitoba, R3M 3S7
www.signature-editions.com

for Joe

Contents

III. The right to bear fangs

What can be done, if our sight lacks absolute power
to devour objects ecstatically, in an instant,
leaving nothing more than the void of an ideal form,
a sign like a hieroglyph simplified
from the drawing of an animal or bird?

— Czeslaw Milosz

I.

Advisory

A bear can smell food ten miles away

Quick! Hide the covert listening devices, the infrared snooper scopes.

Like a shot, Rosalind Franklin, traveller to Oz and British scientist,
writes up her wet-B form data on March 17, 1953.

> The cuttlefish's lunch,
> a large prawn, hangs around with some big brass, muttering, "I see,
> I see," unmindful of the fugitive pursuer passing by unevenly among
> agitated prawns. The bear takes a second look round the middle of the
> beach, touches down on the pale emerald borders, as if translating "on
> the lam" into eastern language. The clam tats, juggles and begs. The
> cuttlefish shoots out her rasping tongue, her dolly diapers, slices a piece
> of lime, and sucks her sup, while the bear, not much liked in the North,
> adjusts his paws and grabs the unbelieving form, and with good appetite,
> rolls it in his mouth, like some firm, chewy candy.

In April of 1953, James Watson and Francis Crick
announce their discovery of the DNA model,
an idea at which Franklin had intuitive guesses, but never published.

On the other side of the Atlantic, "Who's on first"—the catcher
with the most home runs miscalculates, suffers semi-seizures,
and trails off, like love personified, in teensy amounts of typesetting
widths.

A way before

She loved to sleep
and wake up when she'd slept
around the corner, too.
Near the cop station
on Saturday as usual.
Sometimes she'd
have had three winks
and might have been
dozing when she dreamt
all the way, trying to sleep
on Friday and wake up
on Sunday morning but didn't.
She was still beautiful
while she slept scraping
the wall behind the bed
with her knuckles—
not actually remembering that—
the only place she could go
for as long as she wanted. It
might have been the same
night she stretched
and yawned and pulled
down the blinds and woke up
on a Monday twenty-six
years later.

A woman reads

A woman reads a book as she walks her black poodle in the park.
If the poodle falls off the side of that hill, she will not know.
Oh, she'll be too busy looking for clues to the crime story she's reading.
Just maybe the poodle will pretend to fall,
and the woman won't know it is fibbing.

Afterwards

Maybe because the mass of old trees
was not visible from the house
the only signs of life
flourished in the modest flower
of my imagination

The old house   run-down and peeling
stirred uncomfortably like a restless bird
in the heat-exhausted sky
The minutes shut in their concentration
the table returning
to tree with my profuse admiration

Most of the melody would go
in the height of that stumbled-across summer
All the wrong shoes and sandals
the accepted offer of a ride
the abandoned furniture
Not even a fan or photographs
on the table to overcome my embarrassment
The hurts came
at night   one after the other
not just along with the crazy mail
which did no harm
when the season changed

And we drank the evening lying
in that solitude   united
by the full length of our denials
because   unlike the tears
when the pilgrims reached their destination
afterwards the house opened inside

April morning at Thorncliffe Park

Sixteen, the number, is what one sees on the wall:
darkness stepped into the mirror and stayed all week.
Again and again a season is born. Some days it's hard
to shake off doom and gloom, as thunder peals
and shoos remnant winter birds coasting into
the leafless branches.

It's spring, the thin rain
relentless, the fog curtaining tenement windows,
and, down below, the cars and trucks on the highway,
even the tail of The Don that skews through the trees.
The day's mucky enough in black, brown, and grey,
with the constant rolling of rocks in the clouds.

Whatever. Chekhov says
poems shouldn't be riddled with the commonplace.
Until the moment when the new moon arrives,
there is just darkness. That's all there is to it. Who cares
if morning falls and the sun refuses to come out,
and all you can see from east to west is one
infinite blur, your neighbour's laundry
hung out on the balcony, pinned end to end?

Whoever invented this morning
must be one grumpy soul, like a rabid bat descending
to disaster, or some rattled snake who tells
in-your-face stories of cotter-pin retrofits to foil raccoons,
or past-its-due-date-muscle-enhancing drugs for a heavenly
body. Satan's cruel, if funny: why else willingly
let tedium sit without grounding a squirrelly day like no other?

Assignations

Newly orphaned, the images demanded
expression in body language; they wanted meaning
in every possible way, as if caught and held up in the light.
"Lose yourself," someone intoned.
There was disdain for their (presumed) shallowness,
the way in which they improvised their ill-fitting uniforms,
no place more hostile than those places shrouded
by a thick cloud of clichés. Yet, they were constantly
making sand and stone, waiting for the moment
pigs would fly, sealing their characters in tiny rooms
with no food or water, peeling Adam's tags off
those who came before. For how could they not
remember the generation which preceded them,
the wall of memory running from ceiling to floor,
the light skimming through the narrow window,
the suss of the river in the underbrush,
the pulsing, breaking birth of singular astonishment.

Ay

Am/is/are. Ako/kami ay siya/sila.
I/we am/is/are s/he/them.

Once upon a time, I was.
We were. We left and we returned.
We stayed for a very long time.
Our thoughts disappeared.

We filled our brains with new thoughts.
Appearance means the self showing.

We watched television a lot.
Anxiety reveals nothing.

We went to the movies.
The more we turn away from nothing,
the more it holds out.

We spoke in tongues.
Speech lets us see what is being talked about.

We looked and looked.
In the midst of beings, we slip away from ourselves.

We painted our dreams. We held out for nothing.

We photographed our thoughts for contrast and comparison.
They doctored the evidence.

We separated the abstract from the concrete.
They said it would limit our style.

We piled up words.
Hoarded, packed them into our eyes and ears.
Smoked rhythms out of sentences.
Fused language and sound.

They said it was a mistake.
They erased our words.
We will begin again.

Chronology

The prosecution has docketed him for designation as a dangerous criminal offender.

His alleged offenses include armed robbery conspiracy, assault with a shotgun, assault/failure to remain, possession of a prohibited weapon, assault causing bodily harm, and weapons dangerous;

between the ages of 12 and 17, he had 22 criminal convictions, including six for assault and four for weapons;

As an adult, he has been convicted 19 times, including six for assault, three of which involved peace officers; 18 of his convictions occurred during his nine probations;

At 22, was arrested with an unloaded sawed-off shotgun in his vehicle;

At 22, drove a stolen car into a 65-year-old cyclist, killing the man instantly;

At 21, punched a man in the face, then shoved him off the road;

At 20, driving while drunk, and accosted by the police, he kicked out the cruiser window and tried to flee arrest;

At 19, evaded a R.I.D.E stop in a stolen vehicle and was caught after a police chase;

At 18, threw a brick through the front window of a local home;

At 18, threw a knife at a man's head;

At 18, assaulted his girlfriend and threatened to kill their baby;

At 17, bit a teacher on the arm after punching his girlfriend and another girl in the head;

At 14, put his mother's missing cat in a microwave;

At 12, while at a youth detention centre, asked a supervisor what would happen to him if he killed someone, and whether it would be painful to kill someone by stabbing them in the back with a pair of scissors;

At 12, was obsessed with guns, death, war, rebellion;

Between the ages of 6 and 12, was moved from foster homes to group homes;

At 6, was placed by his mother with Children's Aid because she couldn't deal with his destructive behaviour;

At 6, set 15 fires, including one in which a child suffered third-degree burns;

At 6, at a psychiatric assessment, told a doctor he wanted to shoot his mother's boyfriend when he got older because he frequently punished him, ordered him to kneel in a corner for long periods and hit him with a stick;

At 5, used a lighter to set ablaze the clothes of two playmates, including an infant sleeping in a playpen.

Before he was a year old, his father died in a police chase.

Countdown

1

Heavy clouds sail low through the raging battle
in that ancient place sighted from the hills.
Time parcelling old fires
carries what remains of the disputed order.

The seasons sit pure in their extremes.
Variations of folded nights,
object and image transporting significance—
nothing will pass through the darkening radiance.

Too late to uncrumple the world of silences,
shifts of discord,
the quiet lies waving at a distance.
In the morning, burning sands will reveal
the imagined diminishing surface of water.

2

Watch out for the moon.
Expect bad weather.
Fish scales foretell a bad storm.
Moods— like pressure-system winds—
may last for days.

An old backing wind
shapes earth and expected news
as buoyant water hangs unsteady in midair.
Most wisdom never navigates backwards
but moves clockwise on the odd day.

River waters run regnant with shiver,
skim through squall and inconstant billows,
stay inside the solace of a sudden stir,
seek harbour from the gathering runt.

3

Every salt-laden tree
can sting cheeks,
like the subtle teasing stress
of touching grasses or green surf.

4

History is a witch that turned—
stopped and hastened,
enticed—
beckoned memory.
Later, it said, not then, not now,
turning the moment over and over.

Here, it offers blare and spill,
a flood of canvas.
The willing that looks like belonging.
The story of someone—
some people—
climbing out of a pit,
bare arms and feet clawing into effaced rock,
sliding over probability.

Designations

Extremely hungry birds bit off words in the old campus,
in the country whose vegetables were planted in the middle of nowhere,
agitated by the gossip caused by a shoe found outside the front
chamber where the Latin scholar refused to thaw iced scones.

It was time for sweet corn, the water was warm and without river current,
even the good birds had the urge to join, fired up by the proposal
to raise nothing and to put meaning back into circulation.
They gathered round the pack horse like wild cats in comical capers,

each one an expert in pompously inflated language,
each marked by class distinction, each obstinate and vexatious
and uncompromising. They knew thought was the foundation
on which depended all that came later. By sheer force of thought,

they finessed the red brown soil with their duplicity,
knowing that not everyone is set for an outburst,
but would rather tiptoe round the emotional centre,
knowing that the heartless with swords in tents ruff and play the edges.

They buried words in rows of exactness,
kneading each small, biting letter in the way of suffixes,
congealing each riddle with subtle distinctions,
willing each word to be second-to-the-last.

Disquise

i

She has a reputation of having begun her life
in the repetitive dervish of hesitations
of one who is usually quite serious, possessing
the tenacity to numb herself with the quotidian,
by cleaning her house too much—
developing a genius for conspicuous consumption
of borax, dissipating fungus with unconscious cruelty,
with lovage annihilating ants in her bed of phlox.
Her acid rendition of tautness matches the delicacy
with which she approaches what she cannot decipher
with aplomb, her lack of empathy for human beings
who are not so perfect—whom she dismisses
without the artifice or scoffing inflection
of those who believe they have no guile.

ii

Lack of guile is replaced with pushiness—good
strategy when having tea with your neighbour, the one
whose breeding, wealth and power are almost three
sides of the same coin, whose front and back and birl
produce the most startling rhetoric of isolation,
like old belongings hidden in a friend's closet
and completely forgotten, until finally the walls must be
replastered having run up the back garden.
Here you are in love with opposites and waiting
with tremendous trauma for that star of rupture,
an almost believable outbreak of neuropathy,
as if you were listening to the same phone
conversation, yes, the same voice, the same ears
the same appetite for "thought of the week."

iii

Week Three, we need to hold some people accountable.
Here's something else to mull over: the unwelcome
consequences of thinking outside the box, a winding
crown at one o'clock, some good clean and nasty fun
while the status quo shirks the pairing of particulars.
The people are overworked, if you know what I mean.
They don't need to be talked about behind their backs.
Give them a break, give them a laugh, a slap
on the arm. Forget all that talk about changing
the world. All you need is a fascination
with the community's best interests, be it
sacred rituals or Balzac's *Lost Illusions*
or making transitions from small to smaller,
or doing one thing well until the earth disappears,

iv

disappears into the latticework, the son of a
bee who looked like a man, two pylons removed
from the pragmatic and the moderate, whose idea
of gardening was to gack it and whack it, hedge
on sight. Look at the lawns of Toronto! Dandelions
taking over the astroturf of Rosedale and Moore
Park, hopping all the way to Forest Hill, way past
the school of prepositions, air-bound in the reticulate
haze of the LCBO's old train station, the exemplary
sons and daughters who are still living with their biological
fathers and mothers, as if to taunt the law of gravity,
as if there was no other way to live, as if it will keep
them from obsessing about their bodies, or getting
wrinkled in the rain while fussing about their fears.

v

Fears, like some treatise on toxic love, diminish
enjoyment, root and transfix what is wishboned
to the next day, when the good old boy has to answer
his detractors, put forward his many winning qualities,
his appetites, his enthusiasms, like the other day when
he had to argue to place himself on higher ground,
set out some fancy plates for their snob appeal,
remember the sign of the times, the obtuse way he fended
off culpability, phosphorescence emanating from those
blue eyes, as if he registers suffering, or feels
affection for the dark moods of gesture,
the desolate and melancholy iconography of pain,
the postcards sent post-haste to a passel of friends,
to exact attention: here, there was no engagement.

vi

Engagement is for the meticulous, abandoned
in the narrative of loss. Once upon a time there was
a standard-issue credible man hoping for a better future;
by the third page, he was suffering a significant
susceptibility to amassing time, space, experience,
as if he could gather it all in a fitted sheet. In the absence
of lasting remedies, someone or other gave him
a memory, sighs and groans before birds began
to twitter, the photograph before there was a camera,
the dark end of the street before the illumination of twilight,
an unfortunate urge to resist dreams, to burrow
imagination in the ruin of transgressors and occupation,
and, yes, confident he could create balance in the well-lighted
places, couldn't imagine he could collect words before why.

vii

Why, there's only one thing more sacred than man
because the knees are first to go. Under the terms
of engagement, all phenomena are a series of occurrences.
It remains to be seen when a moment's hesitation
can betray allegiances. She could get more things
that she wants if she played the ethics right. For one,
she should be wary of giving too much information.
She could also cultivate a gift for minding her own business.
Or develop calculated and measured phrasings
for carrying out conversation. Of course, there is grievance
enough to cause unhappiness, as when there's
little music to push the plot along, when news becomes
ornament and she runs out of excuses to shock,
"We don't get it" is how everything turns back to normal.

Ends as it begins

> "Basically, the world is made to end up in a book"
> —Mallarmé

There was a life that took me over as if it knew my proper path—
whether or not I liked the one my zodiac sign dictated— the turns
and twists of my so-ordinary frame of mind and behaviour,
which rode the edges of words, the texts and subtexts
in the conversations of others I thought worthier, those who had heft,
who spoke as if they really meant
what they said, and, having said it, seemed profound. So
I skimmed the world's highways, hemming and hawing
and aahhhing, so tickled to believe *this*
was what living meant, taking the faces of the famous
as writ, their actions as my own, their breath my peroration.
Owning them, I could not have been happier because this
was not the darkness when my eyes closed, nor the spaces to be filled
when they opened; *this* was the life I should be living.

Following Turner

Through the doors of Janus,
in the museum exhibiting Turner, Whistler and Monet
caught in a London blizzard, the darkness
lopes across towers, edges of windows, derelict buildings,
the old bridges spanning the Thames.

Turner, master English painter, neatly snatches light
emblazoned on the horizon, hell on the periphery
of a burning building.

Whistler, diffident, grieves, as if the gaze of the ailing woman
by the window never left him, the trail of her long robe
convoluting the spires, melding with the fog, the gathering
of night.

His sombre strokes spill coal dust into crevices, crags, the cobalt
nimbus folds, the spiralling, swirling spumes
of tobacco factory chimneys.

The distant palazzos of Venice mock
Monet's oils of purple-magenta stone walls,
their intricate, winding lines trapping the orange shadows
of ambergris water before dusk,
before knowing,
before redemption,
before the world began.

II.

Little moments

0.4 Interpretation of John Cage's 4:33"
A seminal composition without a single note

[   ]
[   ]
[   ]
[   ]
Leave the stanza,
[   ]
[   ]
[   ]
[   ]
Switch off the sound
[   ]
[   ]
[   ]
[   ]
system. Read on.
[   ]
[   ]
[   ]
[   ]

Okay, I am depressed.

I am tired,
reverse,
leave the stanza.
Disneyland left.

Leave the paragraph.

Get in the right frame
of mind.

Ask the musicians
to turn the pages of the
score sheets after each
of the three movements.

Switch off
the emergency silence.

1:4 Interpretation of John Cage's 4:33"
A seminal composition without a single note

[Thought he was adored father and best pal]
[avid angler waiting for The Big One]
[enjoyed his family, was cruel]
[spent more time cultivating his reputation]
Leave the stanza,
[A collector fully loaded with antiques]
[filled his days counting]
[looked at time through his dual-zone watch]
[slept like a cuckoo]
Switch off the sound
[Outspoken supporter of community values]
[walked to her bridge classes in darkness and all weathers]
[to affirm the city is a safe and friendly place]
[she is remembered for many kindnesses]
system. Read on.
[He was cold, she was wise, they decided years ago]
[that their remains would be donated]
[for medical research and study]
[their ashes interred in a common plot]

Okay, I am depressed.

I am tired,
reverse, leave the stanza.
Disneyland left.

      Leave the paragraph.
      Get in the right frame
      [of mind].

Ask the musicians
to turn the pages
of the score sheets
after each
of the three movements.

Switch off
[the emergency silence].

24 Interpretation of John Cage's 4:33"
A seminal composition without a single note

[You would do well to remember that courage and confidence]
[are not by themselves enough to guarantee success]
[either in your personal life or at work]
[but you have a right to believe what you believe]
Leave the stanza,
[Solar and planetary activity will tell you]
[what it's like to have several people counting on you]
[you seem to be of the opinion that if you ignore a problem long enough]
[it will go away and leave you alone]
Switch off the sound
[Partners and colleagues will tell you otherwise]
[but common sense seems to be lacking at the moment]
[you may have to learn from painful experience]
[you need to earn more or spend less, or both]
system. Read on.
[If things keep coming up at home and in the office, you know]
[what it means. You have to realize that there is no such thing]
[as coincidence, no matter how random events may appear]
[the next bill could be the one that breaks you]

Okay, I am depressed.

I am tired,
reverse,
leave the stanza.
Disneyland left.

Leave the paragraph.

Get in the right frame of mind.

    Ask the musicians
to turn the pages
of the score sheets after each
of the three movements.

Switch off
the emergency silence.

3:4 Interpretation of John Cage's 4:33"

A seminal composition without a single note

[Today: Chance of flurries]
[Overnight: Chance of flurries]
[Tomorrow: Chance of flurries]
[A mix of sun and cloud]
Leave the stanza,
[A 30% chance of flurries turning to rain]
[Wind southwest gusts to 60 km/h]
[A few cloudy periods]
[Otherwise sunny]
Switch off the sound
[A 40% chance of flurries]
[Showers]
[Mostly cloudy]
[Flurries redeveloping]
system. Read on.
[Showers clearing]
[Wind southwest gusts to 60 km/h]
[Flurries changing to periods of rain]
[Tomorrow flurries and local snow squalls]

Okay, I am depressed.

I am tired,
reverse,
leave the stanza.
Disneyland left.

Leave the paragraph.

Get in the right frame of mind.

Ask the musicians
to turn the pages
of the score sheets
after each
of the three movements.

Switch off
the emergency silence.

4:4 Interpretation of John Cage's 4'33"
A seminal composition without a single note

[Horses: box stall avail.]
[Clean, quiet, reasonable]
[Retirees welcome, 15 mins NE]
[Busy hunter barn requires F/T or P/T grooms]
Leave the stanza,
[Eng. bulldogs, puppies]
[shots, papers, microchipped parents]
[on site call 911-555-5555]
[suitable for show or breeding]
Switch off the sound
[Hot tub 2004 model never been used]
[still wrapped, ozonator, dual pumps]
[11HP waterfall aromatherapy, cover]
[cost $11K sacrifice $5K]
system. Read on.
[Fridge—a beauty!]
[+ nice stove washer dryer]
[dishwasher freezer cook top]
[wall oven—best offer]

Okay, I am depressed.

I am tired,
reverse,
leave the stanza.
Disneyland left.

Leave the paragraph.

Get in the right frame
of mind.

Ask the musicians
to turn the pages
of the score sheets after each
of the three movements.

Switch off
the emergency silence.

Grief

It is grief that holds us back—
drupes of apricot shielding the sockets of our eyes,
stones holding gates that guard timorous flanks—

piping on a bone wanting to sing a sad thread of stories,
past a row of fear shadowing the noise on the highway,
pipe of pipits slight and risible, without precedent, without

justification, like obvious holes needing a stopper.
what is wrong with a record being beaten?
It is just a deduction that hits back

and completes a journey. All things considered,
regret is but a plan to get from A to B
in the quickest time by the shortest route.

Hyperqraphia

*To the girl who wrote a ten-page letter to her parents
while they were in the room*

You are like Thomas Henry Huxley who wrote
he was too much of a skeptic to deny the possibility

of anything. Watching you is like watching someone
switch off a light, not knowing it causes a surge

in temperature of more than 4,000F, which causes cracks
in the filament, which is why lights so often go pop

when switched on. Especially when winter solstice
is underway, when winter officially starts in Greenwich,

England, at 7:04 a.m. today, the shortest day of the year,
when the earth is closer to the sun than it was at the summer

solstice, 91,000 million miles, compared to 94,000 million miles,
which is why the light is still going strong in the light bulb

at the headquarters of the Livermore-Pleasanton Fire
Department in California after being switched on in 1901.

Kipling's stories

Kipling brought with him a sack of long talk,
she, a sack of cat's tongues. He said she'd never

leave the room alive. So it was. With perfect clarity,
they gestured for a glass of water, took the bodies

from under their clothes, human beings made in the image
of God. They laid the dead on their sides. It was all

they could do to cast off those whose mouths were wide
open, remove from them the smell of their Cadillac.

The unlucky ones, those who could absorb it all, those
who were possessed, would be listening to Kipling's stories.

First, the tempter disguised as the serpent, then the serpent
disguised as the apple, then the apple disguised as the worm.

"Git away from me!" Kipling spoke as if he'd learned
a foreign language, his arms parallel across the highway,

the woman running parallel to the American border.
They made familiar little noises, like the man in the moon,

as though something was being drawn out from their throats.
"I ain't his keeper," she crowed. "God has a memory," he said.

Little moments

But few are willing to put up
anything certain about certain people
who are notoriously quiet,
don't keep diaries, don't even
write letters. When they want
to highlight something, they leave it
unmarked. What is worrisome is
trying to learn to see how
they close the frame, so the shapes
disappear. You've got to have
a lot of patience with these people.
We don't know much about them.
It's like nobody even bothered
to know, you know.
But that's a good thing. They're like
margins at the centre. When you put
them together, they squabble
but don't speak, even after
prolonged stretches of nimble
cat-and-mousing. It's not like
nobody did anything. Some of us
put ourselves right out there.
They draw against the grid, push
the same story, mount all the parades.
Timing is everything. It's all about
standing in profile, about being careful
of long shots. It's not just about
what they say, it's more about
being lucky. They don't define too much.
Or agonize over mirrored meanings.
They take their shapes but don't eat
any. They go through their show. They
know where to put the sun.

Lost

Look at the little girl left
in the middle of everything,
a market full of stalls,
among okra and eggplant,
catfish and river eel,
ground pork sausaged in veiny belly skin,
beef hanging raw, tripe
rife with dung, forgotten in the dry goods,
among pulses and lentils,
deep where bales of old textile
and ropes and gunnysacks
hurtled her in the dark recesses
of an afternoon fraught with summer's
sorcery, among horses, and paper mâché dolls,
peasant women kerchiefed from the sun,
their long black hair holding a thousand
possibilities.

Manifests

There are languages that leave invisible chances,
slow knolls featureless between the tossing underfoot,
the backstreets of those damned to hell for all eternity.
When they can, they extract the maximum advantage
from speeding wind, as if to exact drift.
We take with us all the frozen poses of duty, the biting,
pinching snarls of doubt, the temper of irrationality, we
negate the measured assertions of our reversed roles
pinned to the blurred white night. It is unlikely
we can decipher all codes to the map of words,
where the site of the carnage vanished,
where what really matters happened,
the sequence after the pummeling and scarring,
the terrain where live the culturally and denominationally bounded.
Sometimes all we need is a finely tuned ear to catch
the crumble of rusk in milk or the chilblain in flip-flops
or the soul pressing seed in the furrow, some Yeatsian vision
offering just what we need at just the right moment.

Morning ritual

The night left a single
drop

on the rusted railing,
for the resident

swallow
to scoop

up
for its morning nip.

At Mass on Mother's Day

A mother carries
her broken son in her arms
to sit in the pew.

Nest, a bird awakes

Teasing the finer points of webbing white,
the bird wakes up in her nest, flaky arteries.
Solitary company to slant of sky,
she flits and rides a tuft of leaves.

The bird wakes up in her nest. Flaky arteries
in breaths of happiness, dry tooth in a twig,
she flits and rides a tuft of leaves,
a ripple of light descending on a breeze.

In breaths of happiness, dry tooth in a twig,
she peeks at a world released,
ripple of light descending on a breeze;
below, love screams in stubborn trees.

Octet for Gioachini Rossini

"In silence I will lament my bitter fate."
—*Metastasio*

In his native country
the stories are perfect
the flaws completely disposable

What follows the plodding striver
is extraneous to the subplot

He feels for his villains
for the pedophile drawn through the eyes
of his loving mother for the drug addict
who has found the Lord for the church ladies
waiting to have fun in their old age
for the pin-up model's thrill of victory

When walls are about to be struck down
best to emulate the sound the groove and the tempo
when people knew what was taboo
when things were neither easy to get
nor convenient to make
nor noticed by the writer
who drew his readers sympathetically into the minds
of villains feeling the forbidden sources
of those who hunt for squirrel loaded for bear

Old alphabet character

Death Valley is below this number that turns back
to zero and ratchets saloon patrons' running totals
in a trig function that could dismay a deity.

But if you catch it with a flugel sound—Mayday!
The hide-hair link is awesome, more generous than
a Jacuzzi joint, way cooler than typing speed,

a charged atom up the creek without a smidgen
of snake squeeze, like ocean hue enjoying a mystery
that comes together as a whole, all the way from Lao Tzu.

Once upon a time

Once upon a time a friar made the sign
of the cross. He saw that terror would do

no more harm, was caught and consumed in the sacrifice.
The man who witnessed was pleased, and, bending over, said

it was the worst blight you could wish on someone,
how all the good would balance it in the end, as should a cigarette

ad in the back page of a magazine. Even the cattle
in the barn called it a bad habit to linger too long

in the middle of your fall. You could tear the wolf off
the creeping tree, the acrid, gassy smell of it: luck's

never free even if things just happen to you; just say sit
to it, and, with peace and patience, all will be forgiven.

Otolith

On the crater's edge, an ovine whine relieved
the silence with a courteous hat flip, then
solidified like an unwell cheese.

They fished for Arctic cod in the circular current
of a polynya but felt very bad about the benefit
of tilting the nerve of hodgepodge sweat
in the elliptical season. If the ice cover
keeps disappearing, then the young cod
will have no ice to hide in.

From the beginning, the frost had a peculiar glow,
like the long slithery end of a riddle, an intuition
of long-ago nimble insurgents fasting in spoils,
a punch-in-the-gut sound of many dead demons
in a burial cavern. Otolith, the cod's earbone,
so much like the stump of a tree, grows a new ring every day.
The width of the ring a guide to the growth rate
of any fish. For a bit of inspiration, it sings metrical feet
in incubation—Boreogadus saida, keystone species,
fish that binds the whole ecosystem
like the last Greek letter, a suckle succumbing
to gravity, a not unusual thing or event in a Yukon town
where once it was -63°C.

Paper safari

i

· ·

Far into the bush,
grassy hummocks
lead to the hidden paths.

ii

· ·

Between us
and the elephant—only
a hush, a shiver.

iii

· ·

With respect and awe
treat rhinoceros or
they will kick your butt.

iv
· ·

Out of bushveld
two elephants crash
into the quick of river.

v
· ·

While six, seven impalas
soft-shoed, clicked their hooves,
cameras ooh.

vi
· ·

Leave the pool quickly—
let the elephants dip, lick,
they so love water.

vii

· ·

Best for scanning zebras
in hot savannah:
dawn, early evening

viii

· ·

Shaded by
marula trees, grass knoll guard over
life and death of prey.

ix

· ·

Lions prowl:
Male, female eye each other,
ignore human eyes.

x

· ·

Kudus
blend into the underbrush—
450 kilos lost in dark.

xi

· ·

Fresh hippo tracks,
a Sherman tank, fear
on two short legs.

xii

· ·

Temp in high 30s,
no one, not even wild prey,
will sit in the sun.

xiii
. . . .

Waterbuck grates head
against dead root, wanders veldt
treks disdainfully.

xiv
. . . .

Into the water plunge
two elephants, flail trunks, heads—
hose, drink, bathe in noise.

xv
. . . .

On the head of a goat,
confess all your sins,
send them to the wild.

III.

The right to bear fangs

Particles of self-assembly

The largest grains come out of pollen from the Forget-me-nots riddling the dirt path on the side of the house. Nehemiah Grew called them "particles of prolifick virtue." The Queen Bee closeted in the blackberry trunk thinks otherwise. She saw the three women transformed into flowers of the field. One of them allowed to stay in her own house at night, but, as day approached, was obliged to return to her field companions again to become a flower. But one time, just before leaving her husband, she said to him: "If you will come this morning and pick me, I shall be set free to stay with you from then on."

And that is what happened.

The Queen believes they're like the perilous young she had stroked in the belly of the tree, their tongues tight, impervious as the carbon wall the exines built to keep their fingerprints on the ice cores, the sediments of lake bottoms. Moisture swells the spores, as if thinking of the trail up ahead, slides snugly into the grommet hole in the blackberry trunk.

In a few decades people can order eident honey by touching the base of the tree and never ask: "What does it look like?" The openings are critical. In the story, the flowers being exactly alike, how did the husband recognize his wife? No clue except the surface could be a breakthrough.

In the day, I spend a lot of time with my mouse and keypad. I narrow down the season when the rose comes out. Borne on the wind. Its expectation of touch. Carried by bees, other insects. The grammar, vocabulary and style of recognition, the simple-to-intricate ways of coming and going, the narrative of heave and shape. Find out if the hard swell is compatible with the stigma.

Snowfall

*(as seen from a window frame sparking
a particular stimulation in the past that will be shuttered
and blinded in April)*

Two squirrels race across the wood-ratcheted fence
while apple trees stand like Christ's sentries
behind stucco houses unmoved by last night's snowstorm
making no distinction between a fib and a lie
or a small pool or a hot tub or an herb garden
or that thing which houses the mind gives rise to the mind
to be made flesh any more than words can fit into a truck
same same that comes here every Sunday at dawn
a bridge over a pass a cheap hack flack who looks
for the good parts in people even when he knows they are not there
forgiving because some could be so blind and not know it
like blind bats with thin fur and webbings and high-pitched shrieks
seeking the shapes of trees and insects wresting pain
out of the flesh the colour blue out of neurons firing
knowing that if they tilted their heads to the right
they'd see the ecliptic plane of the planets along the horizon
contiguous with the rivers and the stones and the rest of the world

Stairway to heaven

Not knowing where to stow our dreams
we climbed up step pyramids with chambers beneath
the street, metal spoons, the stones of eight hundred years

On the scaffold the gardens grew flowers of uncommon name
or broke out into branches of outstretched arms
singing songs without vowels or consonants

We peeked under the stairs and found thousands of bodies
wrapped in bales of bleached muslin
sorted, stacked, heaped one on top of the other

Those who were not privileged were left untouched
to rot, the worms content to pick clean the bones
as we sought out greener gardens

We thought if we pushed the right buttons
we could negotiate our way to heaven
or at least escape to some altered paradise

We travelled the world to seek better opportunities
but each time the stair landing opened up
to fried chicken at gas stations or a gun at the supermart

or oracles predicting news of the vanished
a throng of beggar boys with their empty tomato cans and
girls who will fetch water and firewood forever

At the summit someone said "The cattle and the fish
will meet at the end of time" so we found it improbable
to think of sleep or even to need love songs

Slowly, slowly, we waited by heaven's gate
walking over hot burning coals
but this is a labour-intensive business and one can't expect

the place to be mostly empty and mellow and finished by noon
only that it be white as sugar cubes rattling in tin cans
white as fresh sorrow bandaging the sky

The bear rose

I planted a coiled rose
below the window sill,
watered its roots, stroked
its back, prompted it
to grow fast and strong.
It slept in afternoons,
I know, not growing
shoots or tendrils, just keeping
to itself, burrowing
and murmuring soft
lullabies to lull itself
to sleep, turning and tossing
and mewling about its rosiness
as if it could will itself
to be present in a moment
it could savour, first as bud
then flower. As soon
as it felt its roseate cluster fill,
it arose from the coil, a bearful
of plump ardour, its sweetish
breath suffusing the room.

The cross-hatched elephant

In Chile, I found an elephant
whose hide was etched in squares,
a giant map of hazardous elements
tinkling with erudition.

"Don't say a word." He throws
a die at me, and disappears
in the fabula, a novel of fables,
by turns mystic and speculative.

"Drink, moron." He offers mog
in a hollowed-out leaf, confident
as a fly suspended in disbelief.
"If you choose, choose."

"Protect your illusions. Guard
them like a moth." "If you love
words, temper them with emotion."
"The road to perfection is conceived

neither in miles nor feet."
"In nature, dawn precedes blight."
"Art is ministered neither
by wind nor creed."

"A poem touched by anecdote
invites creation, you must live
with the word." On parting,
he said, "If you choose truth, disembody,"
and flew away with the idea.

The eye of the king

She began her life as a white marguerite,
a serious and capable girl derided,
often humiliated, for her beauty, one
whose exquisite mind and delicacy
were so coiled within, those around her thought
a spiral staircase had more saving grace.
Had they asked the nun who sat with her
in her death cell, or the young soldier
of the firing squad, would they have drawn out
her true self, plain-speaking, pensive,
trying to break free from old habits,
a gamelan dancer given to absinthe who broke
the hearts of various young men
in her temple ritual, a woman afflicted
with a terrible run of bad luck.

The film stopped

And the blonde women and the little man with wheat hanging
over his eyes sat on worn leather chairs splitting from neglect
close to the aisles, emptiness all around.

Pictures of pastel shades, lakes and bright quilted bedspreads
a few murders and barroom brawls
and lovely ladies kissing handsome men

mingled with the sausage-and-gravy-stained floral curtains.
And the little man and the women started growing older,
began to read the titles under the lines.

Lying, cheating, forgery, and betrayal of trust.
They thought the film went too far, opened six inches of their mind
but left their blood heavy and blue.

And the hairy cop in the small locked cupboard was still there
fluorescent in the dark while the buildings were crumbling,
the neighbourhoods poorer, riots breaking out over the cost of bread.

In the shadows something funny happened, as with so many horrible things
The theme music was so melancholy it made them
homesick. Except for their glum resolve to live they had determined

to trust their judgment implicitly, knowing that at first they must
taste nothing, do their best to create a little order, as in the beginning
fill their thoughts with fresh longings

for the crust of snow atop the ice, the opening of oven doors,
a place that has disappeared, the window that looks out to the sea,
the simple interval of a perfect fifth, what doesn't exist anymore.

In spite of everything was it not still true that the longer a bird lived
the more it would have to remember the taste between sweet and bitter,
the infinite regress of sun and rain in the narrow paths,

the return of kindness, wild grass, old wooden houses,
the sails of the herring fleet and the marvelous deeds
of hordes driving earth and water to submission.

The great dying

Up the road sprang a phalanx of criss-crossed vines.
In resolute formation, slender poles of grape leaves
hatched in and out as if to taunt someone's idea of rows
of orange curtains. You haven't heard of the road to erewhon,
the here and now suddenly distant, and the soldiers
demanding proper identification—or else—
that you couldn't reproduce because you'd left behind name, birth date,
and birthplace in your haste.
They allowed you 24 hours to retrieve those lost items.*
Down the road where you came from, a woman thrashed about
like a lobster dropped in a pot of boiling water,
and slumped on a curb, needles on the ground. The thrashing
was not triggered by pain, the soldiers said, but was an escape response.
The sallow men close by, men who had lost the ability to speak
but could tell the difference between dog biting man
and man biting dog, shrugged—they knew nothing.
Documentarists would say that years later greenhouse gases from erupting
volcanoes caused The Great Dying 250 million years ago.

*Caveats: If anyone had opened their spleen they would have found
valuable stem cells that could have aided their healing. Had they left
water in the sun for six hours, they would have had clean water.

The right to bear fangs

October 20—

Is this where civilization begins—
at the confluence of the Don River and Taylor Creek,
where the willow tree breaks the road in three?
      Forks indicate direction:
            whichever you take, I will follow.
                Dogs schooled in obedience
keep tally, study the annulations of roots skeining the banks of the creek,
      run the length of a solar year, scratch the dirt
            off hieroglyphs carved into the limestone stela.

2

Escape hatch 1956: A barrel full of Granny Smith apples
at the mouth of Mt. Pinatubo before it spews out ash
and molten lava, eats a president of the Republic,
drives the Americans out of Clark Air Base,

                    1999: My sister sends over a lahar-
encrusted plastic rock as a souvenir.
                            My father gives me a pen,
      my mother an inkwell, to draw the stringed
pieces of our lives. My mother says the vibrations
of those strings in 26 dimensions imitate the particles
                 of higher, hidden, universes.

3

February 1961:

After years of being leashed to a post in front of our house,
our dog Brownie suddenly develops a distaste for old bones. His growls
become more ferocious. He bites my hand when I feed him.
I end up taking shots in the local infirmary for 21 days.
The needle pricks me in the back like a backstab,
the way a mouse feels when
it is pinned on a mousetrap.

March 2001: His name is Janus, his owner tells me on the elevator. Part-Rottweiler, part Labrador. Except for the dark shadows around his brown eyes, Janus appears gentle, doesn't growl or scowl as humans sometimes do.

Mid-February 1961: Brownie dies
on a leash, his ghost feet limbing into the trees,
kinkling the space beyond us.

4

December 7, 1941:
Preparing for war,
my parents were told to hide
medicine, quinine tablets, calcium tablets,
cod liver oil, powdered milk,
soap, candles.

At one point, during the Second World War, the Penaranda River
flowed with corpses
of men and women bayoneted
by the enemy,
betrayed by local hooded men,
their faces hidden by straw bags, who pointed out
those who aided the guerrillas.

In the years after the war,
although I slept with my siblings under mosquito nets
on matted floors, I felt alone.
I had recurrent nightmares.

I would wake in a sweat in the middle of the night.
Each day I became more and more afraid of the dark.

Once, a woman in white gazed at me
in my half-sleep. The next morning I found out she
was my mother's white dress
hung to dry in the room. It had rained all night.

5

The hardscrabble sky unleashes a storm.

> *April 1994:* In Rwanda, dogs, travelling in packs,
> feed off corpses.

Someone fires the first missile.
The presidential guard and the militia hunt like digger wasps.
The radio blares: "Clean the fields."
"The graves are not yet full."
Men, women, children, whole families.
Gangs shoot, club,
hack with machetes. Rape.
Inside the dead children's pockets,
the bonekeeper finds marbles.

Hard rain wets the noses,
snapped jaws.
Dog tongues loll,
muzzle, paw,
drool, yawp.

6

Six years after apartheid,

        black prisoners are attacked by police dogs

                behind a gold mine dump.

       Three black men

              repeatedly savaged by four dogs

     from the East Rand Dog Unit

         as six white police officers cheer.

7

News items: A white businessman drags a black colleague
behind his truck for six kilometres. A shop owner accuses
a young black girl of stealing, then strips her
to the waist and paints her white.

Response from a radio caller:
"I was very impressed with the way
the dogs worked.
I can honestly say I felt nothing."

8

Human crowds moving under pressure may release forces
　　　　　powerful enough
　　　　　　　　　　to bend steel or topple brick walls.

　　　　　　　　　　　Some Friday in March 1967
　　　　　When a fire hit our neighbourhood, my mother carried
our refrigerator 16 steps down onto the street. With her bare
hands, no questions asked, price tag still stuck on the back. We had been
among the first to make ice cubes in our town.

In a Bicutan holding cell for political detainees in the Philippines,
a female prisoner was forced to lie naked on a block of ice.
They wanted her to spit out the names of her friends.

Scribbled on the sea wall in Old Intramuros, Manila,
behind the ice cream vendors:

DO YOU BARK?
ONLY DOGS PISS HERE.

9

Four months, two, and four—
ages of the children who died when their parents'
log cabin burned to the ground,
a hundred metres from the choppy ocean waters.
Their scrawny dog bayed at the moon,
was spurned, wet and forgotten.
The neighbours' hound remembered other fires,
other burnings.

February 1, 1983, Malambago, Bukidnon:
"Hapa! Hapa!" ("Lay flat! Lay flat!")
A young woman, just turned 18, leaps
to shield her younger brother from a burst
of gunfire on their hut.
                        The paramilitary soldiers
riddle her with bullets
        avenging
                the death of one of their men.

10

To prove his everlasting devotion, a man will buy his beloved
a pavé diamond eternity ring.

Global Witness reports
that rough diamonds generated

> U.S. $750 million in 1999
> exchanged for
> cheap machine guns from former Communist states
> > and American-made landmines.

> Because of these diamonds,
> Memunatu Mansaray, a four-year-old girl from Sierra Leone,
> whose arm was amputated by rebel soldiers,
> > can't eat
> with her right hand, write a letter,
> > pet her puppy, hug her doll.

The Diamond High Council
says it takes about 250 tons of rock,
> sand, and gravel
> to yield one carat of diamond.

> One carat equals a fifth of a gram,
> comes from carubis,
> > the seed of the carob tree.

Posted on the door
of the Kimberly Club, South Africa, 1898:

NO DOGS AND WOMEN ALLOWED.

11

A confederation of dogs by the mouth of the river
learns the alphabet of war,
syllables of destruction.
They talk about war and wealth, fret over
the cultivation of fire, dismembered corpses, bombed-out cars,
the significance of statistics.

February 2001: On the Twelfth Night, Sam the dog
leads the pack at the Barkus Parade in New Orleans. He's all red and blue
coattails and feathers, a rhinestone crown and silver ball on his neck.
Struts his stuff with 1000 canines in the French Quarter, stops only
at the stroke of midnight on Shrove Tuesday.

(From the crowd: WHOA, SAM, YOU'RE OUR MAN!)

                    Somewhere in the night, dogs are napped
and crammed into trailers:
                    Labrador retrievers, spaniels, shepherds and their mixes,
                                                    all breeds,
        for puppy mill breeders, dogfight organizers, research labs.

The rosary of houses bears witness.
Tire-scarred tar. Spumes of dust.
Dog collars, leather straps, metal chains.
Bark, if you dare.

12

It happens all the time. In parks
                    across the world.

        A city dog sweeps a squirrel
                    off the grass, corks him to the ground.
        Tail gnawed, hanging by its end,
                    cheek on asphalt.
                            The passers-by
        awestruck.
                    Dog gone into the trees.

The squirrel floats into the clouds   turns into
            a hydroxyl radical. In the ozone layer,
                            it zaps carbon monoxide,
                sulphurous gases,
unburned oil solvents, heavy metals, radioactive materials.

            Back on earth, black dogs gride
their paws on glass.
                Their treacle drills memory onto granite.

The soldiers left

the enemies' hands
nailed to the tables
each body a place setting
as organized as a dinner

The tree of heaven

Genus: Ailanthus altissima

Had the tree stood still, it would not have brought itself trouble.
But it grew roots and branches like an island suffering traumas,
learned to creep up in the air like sin cavorting with a first hint
of richness, its body badderlocking delighted liens, flawed threads
on the neighbour's backyard, breaking and entering the picket fence,
outdoing itself in knotted sedilias, breaching, twining hardy vines
as if there were nothing to crime, or a stye, or the chemist's poison,
attempting without right to pace around the grass, overruling
the more-than-clearly-enunciated signs registered as bylaws, the line
that divides what is obsessed, set as a straight contract condition,
the joyous squeeze-snake of mine and yours, the prickly bush
spreading the sharp abrasions that upset civility.

The way a plague transforms the land

Whenever a plague transforms the land,
life becomes a suffering, the bloom of guilt
gathers around grief and recrimination.

In those towns where death releases
subtle inflections of uncertainty, groups move
in a single file of extreme caution,

leave a latticed glimpse of the horribly wounded,
and, on the wayside, people who've numbed
themselves with routine, their loss a tonal variation

that moves their story forward.
They surge without hesitation or artifice,
through distances and attempts to be humane.

The old man thinks the first part of the movie
is something like the ragged and jagged
pastel ghosts exhausting the placid clouds,

the wretched and the scarred tempered by anticipation.
All those generations of facetious formations
need kindness and a firm consciousness

of being the other if they are to survive.
Their stories' facts would be hard to check, if at some point,
the attempt were made to nail their meaning down.

If they did exist, they were like the cat
in the cage with an apparatus given a fifty-fifty
chance of killing the cat within an hour.

It is a matter of instinct, the proper punctuation
of ideas; it all flows like the dream in the book.
On the evening when the plague ends, the old man

will see the apparitions simultaneously there and not there.
Other viewers will attest they can neither confirm nor deny
the likelihood that such an event occurred.

This day

Kafka said his friend Georg Trakl died
because he had too much imagination, died because
he could not endure the war, helmets, armies, wounded men,
battlefield nurses, the blood that ran
from the wounds the day thousands died—a red cloud,
a furious god.
The people who came after only knew
how to possess and rule
like empires of old
laid waste by rebellion and warfare,
every power grid,
water pipe, bridge, road
and war-related factory targeted.

If they had tried to comprehend,

had they placed themselves as the other
in that other place,

would they have been so inclined to amass
and to claim dominion over everything?

It's not the things we know that hurt us,
it is the things that aren't so.

The spilled blood finds its home,
silently gathers a moonlike coolness
in the willow bottoms.

If they had sought the secret
of the dream
would they have cut it free?

Had they followed its contours would they have reached
the fullness of knowing?

We will set your country back by pulverizing you

Sleep somehow strengthens
memory,
the slow wave that embeds facts and events.

Spindles of
pattern

fret over
and across

the never-ending gusts of arrivals,
leavings,

like tiny shrimptoed krill, surfacing

on water,

stirring up

a turbulence.

Thoughts patter and flow
but may have no more right than
what one allows them.
What really counts are the things
we know. We know
shifts of key and time,

but that may be missing the point.

A stray

thread   wants

to get back

in the loop.

Too long and our heads might be pulled off,

too

short

and

we

might

suffocate.

Transports

The church

People walk on a surf of mist, kick nimbus
clouds tortilebobbinround the spine as they enter the gothic house.
Tense in a rundle they furl entrails
fink heaven and soul to fuss,
loop the spirenest of desire roll, tuft, querl urge to soar
wip and clew and curl haspids on the yellow cake
dog fog of the nuke sky, blur of damp dark dusty fool hiding
behind the hazy muddy nub of Okaye,
rage over the army's air attack
while video footage sullies the swarm with a tour
of buildings, cirrus damaged overground tunnels in a funnel,
muddled with nebulous weapons and ammunition
pile-ups, poother pother screening camp deserted for years.

In the catacombs
there's a faint chill an icy mur nipping
the dead, the dull hard husk of hoar,
murmur of roup, gelid lace of oorie ourie parky poose,
freddo frigoer glossing marbly catarrh,
and, in the distance, frosted glacial shivery
snivels hug clip of cull.

Inside flying arches little girls practise on pointe toes,
boys shoot square hoops, kids play roustabout
among the pews. The pastor says it's the only way
to get around land development.

After the service people pass through a row of jacarandas
jossed with paper and rose buntings, bloom of ash gul knot
moss rois briar bridebuckflush bourbon hugonis.

O Ophelia.
O Columbia. O dogberry. O pedelion.
O cudweed, dwarf polyantha hybrid noisette
whispering mumbo jumbos on the rose campion, tumbling
on roselle, pursing lips on sorrel.

The house

Beside the tall spires a row of rococo-style houses wait
to be habited, and in the back a manse full of holes,
its helmeted owners processing a pack of motorcycles.
On the aha fence a tag of blackbirds guards the face
of a goddess hanging on a tang of etymons.

I told my cousin he's one of many poor.
The house was the greatest bargain this side
of the world, a total banger do-ed up to look contempo—
with oriel windows—an old house backing up a hundred feet
from its front, the burnt mansions left
with their cinders burning as if their time
was not yet up.

It wowed the relatives to see one of their own rise
from the rubble and rebuild this grand house.
But when we went to exit the back door,
the neighbours' houses were cramped
back-to-back, the road narrow and pockmarked,
the sewers sawed-off like the innards
of another world, jasmine bushes crawling over
garage doors and balconies,
the flower clusters dank with the scent of old altars,
their greedy owners allowing us to pick
only the fallen and rusty blooms,
stray bouquets to give to the waifs waiting
to offer them to the mantled woman in white,
the one they called blessed.

The trees

If the fever-trees are drawn with blood
and the shadows hide them, will they plout the weet
of blash, skiff the onding stem?
Plow-mist-of-metres mizzle beetles in the elms,
hide the puff reek and spur of arcus
in the monocots.

Remember rain and its permutations

u	l	a	n	u	l	a	n
l	a	n	u	l	a	n	u
a	n	u	l	a	n	u	l
n	u		a	n	u	l	a
u	l		n	u	l	a	
l	a		u	l	a	n	
a	n		l		n		
u		a		u			
n		l					
			u				

l
an ulan ula
n ulan ulan ulap ulap ulap ulap alapaap ala-paaapp
Figure a cloud that needs airing.

Read blind---f-o-l-l-o-w---y---o---u---r-----e-y-e-s with the spit of dag
pash winddog rone.

Listen to the old woman who wants
to become a philosopher. Are you real or
my invention? Do you exist outside
or inside me? Are you there yet? Are you?
She does not scuff the rabble, the herd of demagogues,
the race of underground elves.

She does not yet know to become a great thinker
she must first be who she is. Do not steal this poem.
This sentence is true if she looked outside
the window. The leaves flutter
because she does not see the wind.
The spider plant inside the sill keeps still
because it wants to think.
Deep and solitary as the stubborn millionaire
who kept 500 peacocks to colour his garden,
whose daughters, forced-fed on broccolini,
abandoned him,
forgot their phone numbers,
eloped with chauffeur and electrician,
like Cain, fleeing the wrath of God,
left his banjo clock
to regulate the dean of student affairs.

Drow in the mountains.
Drink bonducchicotvirgilia
with gin on your breath
the way we adjust
our tongues and tastes, live by our word.
Blacken conduse cumulate eclipses fumuli granules,
obscure the stratus of sunspots,
tarnish our cloud caps,
mix cocktail with nightcap
nubilate one to another

Here is what I seek:

agrimony in antimony, overcast, woolpack
warm, absorbent like grass,
something good in the rain,
a point to return, a quire of questions,
the snell bitter and boreal,

something I could argue
with the fishy frore,
an optimistic starling worried
over the grave escalation of tensed cats hiding in tufted coons.

TTTtttt(hhhhhhhhmmmmmhhh)
gtttsssshhhwwetsssrrgghhhghhhhttssssshhhjj
(hmmmmmhhhhmmmmmm) their hearts sinking when the curtain
rose,
forgetting to floss food particles from their philosophy and wit,
avoiding the tic-tac-trickle of water
the slow ascent of bibulous Marys trying their damnedest
to pirouette,
zigggggggyzagzagzag zapdancing on concrete.

Waiting

What will you do while you're waiting?
Your body narrative lies buried on the coastline,
sand sifting in its loosening segments,
the litter of years, roots and vines, tangling
over its cretaceous sediment, ore seeping tears
in folds of the precipice. You have joined

sand and clay, rock weak and friable, joined,
painted over and blurred, like seaweed awaiting
the illusion of coves and bays the sea tears—
the shales, pale silt of ancient coastline flint,
potter of soft clay on the toe of cliffs and vines,
waves reaching for shore segments,

pressing for affirmation, the intimacy that segments.
Hold for breath. The rood's transfiguration joined
in the empty path of walkers and vines
constantly erases its masks in the waiting.
Yield to appearances that define the coastline.
There's no going back, for sure, despite the tears

of the boy opening his shirt to let tears
of petals fall from his heart—digitalis, the segments
of love, a song to carry you over the coastline,
a call to the moon in hopes it will call back, joined
in the flood of memory, old wounds gushing, waiting
for the rustle of breakers on the reef, the vines

moving words, the map of your deliverance, vines
of the story made up here, any place where it tears,
moves through the details, the hold of grief waiting.
Where you start, anywhere the road segments,
is quite different, the turn is lost, not just joined,
no matter the distance. It grows, recedes to the coastline,

the thread of the story sending notes to the coastline.
More wilderness than life springs from the vines.
A day starts like another, a bird swoops, joined
to the wind as it runes through winter tears,
renders memory visible, its shadow on rock segments.
The bird will deliver the seed to your mouth: waiting

strangely close and joined as you began on the coastline,
no sense in waiting for rain fragments to gather among vines
to find a route that tears in its rivering segments.

Welcome to hell

Photos from Open Wound: Chechnya 1994 to 2003
by Stanley Greene

Welcome to hell, you are lost now.

A telephone wire still dangles from a lamp post
in Prospekt Pobedy, Grozny. In November 1995
rebels were hanged from telephone wires by the Russian infantry.

Zina Asdamirova, 28, propped up on her bed,
hides her torn body, half of it blown away
by shrapnel, beneath a sheet printed with plump red poppies.
The headboard haloes a face lost in thoughts of her brother,
killed while searching for food for his hungry children.

In a triptych mirror: Zina, a single mother and her three children
refracted in a corner of a metal wagon,
courtesy of the Red Cross. The wagon, scorching hot
in summer and icy cold in winter, displays
their hoard of broken bowls, a thermos bottle, empty pickle jars.

1997, a family of seven: wiped out—father,
mother, two girls, three boys—by Russian artillery in 1999.

In downtown Grozny in April 2001: Zelina's face, hidden partly by a
misted glass window after a heavy rain.
Since the death of her child, she thinks she is
already dead herself.

(Except for land mines, trip wires, booby-traps,
the city is largely deserted.)

Wolff on a bed of burdocks

Chance, John Cage says,
      tosses pizzicato
      of dice and coins scratching music from slide whistle

and sarrusophone,

melodic and harmonic fusion
      furling
           and unfurling,

buzzing line,
           rhythm,
and sequence.

Wolff's full text/score for part 10:
"flying,
      crawling
           or possibly
                sitting

                        still."

Wearing tiny wings on their shoulders,
      the musicians
           scat to the aisles in one full swoon.

Performer into listener:
      into composer:
           into performer.

Mute, 4 or 5 ways:
Sound like a smoke signal.
Wood.
      A very slow glissade.

Movement 5 of Burdocks:
Sound of one material

passing through another broken strand
with no flaws.
        Hedge your bets
            on more than one possible outcome.

Xenon

If you know exactly
where you are
you cannot know
exactly where
you are heading
and if you know
exactly how you
are heading
you cannot know
exactly where
you are
Just as
dawn glimmers
in the great
silence
or wind wafts
westward
over far off
bright stars
a cat may be
inside
and outside
the box
at the same
time

You ate my city

I will leave, but I will not stop growing.

You can't say, "There was too much to do in so little time."
Your everlasting sentinels still keep watch
over irrigation channels, grazing areas, footpaths.

You told us, "Give up your rocket launchers, tanks
and machine guns," yet our farmlands whir
with echoes of bounding frags, cluster bombs.

Transparency and accountability hog space
with thin asphalt stirred in huts while the water hazard
in a nearby golf course goes bone dry.

The caddies will be armed, they've been trained
to deal with their own terrible problems, they know
when to hurl lightning bolts to earth.

The past is in us, the rag-wrapped cripples waiting
along the hard points—your legacy of unexploded pucks—
in the skies bleeding the colour of conquest into our rain-fed valleys.

Listen to our prayers rise: the effect will be transformative.
Ordinary people who do small things can rouse
to the salutary promise of the god of prophecy.

At its melting point lead will mix with water.

Zaum

Beyond sense, says Khlebnikov,
Russian philosopher
of the true names of things,
("meta = along with, after,
related to, or transcending")
reality is in the words,
not outside of the words.
A rose is just an idea.
Ideas exist only
when they are described,
expounded, elucidated.

The books in the bookcase
refracted by afternoon
light are not figments of one's imagination:
"All is well that begins well and has no end."

To be the word, to be the victory
over the sun—
the positive and negative shape,
the excluded middle,
line and colour,
post-revolutionary prop
of the futurist opera
fading to an emotional roller-
coaster ride—
like some suffering old horse being urged
to a dead run on a treadmill,
hole within the whole,
not some infinite turn
that withers inside,
and, breathless,

sings songs
over dry bones
wrapped in cerements.

Things exist whether
you name or name them not—
they live in a place
and leave nothing
of themselves behind.

An alphabet for the world

The world began, so they say,
with a noun, and the noun begat a verb,
and the world grew,
begetting nouns and verbs,
permutating in hybrid
combinations, as if the world knew
what it was doing.
Cayo coco, cayo coco,
sol cayo Santa Maria,
holguin, sol rio luna mares,
sol sirenas, sol palmeras,
the sweet sap of mighty maples,
the dark, mysterious places,
the conception, the celebratory
birth of aa, amoeba, bacteria,
the six dots of the Braille cell,
os, plant, protozoa, pneumonoultra-
microscopicsilicovolcanoconiosis,
Rx, zephyr, the pattern of parading
images still to be dreamt,
tactful engagements
with the arranged, the desolate,
the meticulously turned,
pores shining from deep tunnels—
the gold mean number split down
the middle of timelessness, a place
made from scratch, with no history
of solid achievement or potential,
its dark dense gravity a circuit
looking for something important
to peg on, such as luck,
or happenstance, or serendipity,
or favourite card game rules,

like some kind of protection
from those who heard the word
and thought something
was happening, yeah, like
some black stone, to cover
the A's, to keep tongues
tight, trilling in unison.

Notes

Page 2: Quotation excerpted from Czeslaw Milosz's poem, "Esse," in *Selected Poems 1931-2004*, Czeslaw Milosz, Harper Collins Publishers, 2006.

Page 16: Based on "25 and too lethal to be set free," by Bob Mitchell, *The Toronto Star*, B1-2, March 20, 2004.

Page 26: Poetic permutations inspired by John Cage's 1952 composition, *4'33"*, the three movements of which are performed without a single note being played. The score includes three silent movements, each of a different length (30", 2'23", 1'40"), but when added together total four minutes and thirty-three seconds. The content of the composition is meant to be perceived as the sounds of the environment that the listeners hear while it is performed, rather than merely four minutes and thirty-three seconds of silence. Cage uses the "silence" of the piece as an aural "blank canvas" to reflect the dynamic flux of ambient sounds surrounding each performance. Commenting on his piece, Cage says: "Silence is not acoustic. It is a change of mind. A turning around." On the other hand, he says, "Music is continuous. It is only we who turn away." Culled from: http://en.wikipedia.org/wiki/4'33".

Video performance by David Tudor (1952) on http://www.youtube.com/watch?v=HypmW4Yd7SY

Acknowledgments

I've read parts of the manuscript with my poetry group which saved me from the sludge and sloth of my excesses. So my thanks go first to Ruth Roach Pierson, Maureen Harris, Sue Chenette and Julie Roorda — gifted poets all — who were especially generous with their comments and sage advice.

To Paolo Chikiamco, editor and publisher of Rocket Kapre Books, for including "Designations," "Stairway to heaven," and "You ate my city," in Rocket Kapre's ebook, *Ruin and Resolve (2009)*.

Many thanks to my editors Stan Dragland, for his thorough reading and incisive pen, and Carolyn Marie Souaid, for making my collection look good. And to Lina Kim for helping set up the manuscript for publication.

I am lucky to have my daughters — Jenny, Patricia Kim, Isobel and Rani — who, in their big and small ways, continue to inspire me to keep the poetic juices flowing.

And finally, I must thank Joe Rivera, for being there with his love and constant support.

Patria Rivera

Patria Rivera's first poetry collection, *Puti/White*, was short-listed for the 2006 Trillium Book Award for Poetry. She has also published *The Bride Anthology* and co-authored *Weathering: An Exchange of Poems*. Her poetry is featured in *Perspectives in Ideology*, and in Elana Wolff's *Implicate me: short essays on reading contemporary poems*. She has received fellowships from the Writers' Union of Canada, the Banff Centre for the Arts, and the Hawthornden Castle Writers' Retreat. Rivera holds a journalism degree from the University of the Philippines, and hopes to live each day—24 hours/1,440 minutes/86,400 seconds—burning clean and without dripping. She lives with her family in Toronto's east end.